Introduction to Prolog

WITHDRAWN

Essex County Council

Many libraries in Essex have
facilities for exhibitions
and meetings —

enquire at your local library
for details

Computer Language Handbooks

Introduction to Prolog

Brian Walsh

Pitman

Computer Handbooks

The complete list of titles in this series and the Pitman
Pocket Guide series appears after the Index at the
end of this Handbook. The Publishers welcome
suggestions for further additions and improvements
to the series. Please write to Peter Brown at the
address given below.

PITMAN PUBLISHING LIMITED
128 Long Acre, London WC2E 9AN

A Longman Group Company

© Brian Walsh 1986

First edition 1986

British Library Cataloguing in Publication Data

Walsh, Brian
  Introduction to Prolog — (Computer language handbooks)
  1. Introduction to Prolog (Computer program language)
  I. Title   II. Series
  005.13'3   QA76.73.P7

ISBN 0 273 02694 1

Printed in Great Britain at the Bath Press, Avon

Contents

The co-workers and students of Brian Walsh would like to express their deep respect and affection for the memory of this dedicated and generous colleague who died while this book was in the final stages of preparation.

Publisher's note

If the author had been in a position to write his own acknowledgements, he would doubtless have wished to thank his colleagues for their support and encouragement. Dave Sherratt suggested a number of useful improvements, and Chris Wooff proofread the book and provided information on VM/Prolog.

How to Use this Handbook

Prolog is a declarative language whose name is derived from **pro**gramming in **log**ic. The emphasis is placed on *what* the program tasks should be, rather than on *how* these tasks should be executed. Prolog obeys the logic rules of First Order Predicate Calculus, and in addition, contains the necessary features to function as a complete programming language. This Handbook describes the features of 'core' Prolog, which is very close to Edinburgh Prolog, and is the basis of many implementations such as C-Prolog, DEC Prolog, Prolog-2 and York Portable Prolog.

Appendix 1 gives additional details for Micro-Prolog and IBM's VM/Prolog.

Conventions used in this Handbook

Prolog program statements will appear in **bold** type.

Comments in programs appear between **/*** and ***/** thus

   /* This would be a comment */

The Prolog interpreter indicates that is it expecting user input when it displays the **?—** symbols.

A Gentle Introduction to Prolog

A number of computer terms such as 'function' are used in this section which relate to languages such as BASIC. They are not normally used in Prolog but are included to ease the introduction of new Prolog terms. Definitions of all the Prolog terms are provided in Appendix 2.

The following descriptions of example programs assume that a Prolog interpreter has been loaded into the computer (*see* Running Prolog Programs on p.9).

Example programs

The interpreter prompt **?–** means that it is expecting a goal. That is, something which requires proving true or false, and the system will respond with a corresponding **yes** or **no.**

Supplying a goal to a Prolog program is the means of telling the system to execute it.

Assume the following program has been loaded:

sum(X,Y,Z) :– Z is X+Y.

and the interpreter prompts the user with

?–

The first input is

?– sum(1,2,A).	Note the full stop at the end of the statement. To send it press RETURN.
A=3	This is the result. To continue press RETURN.

yes
?–sum(15,12,X).
X=27
yes
?–

3

The program can be thought of as a function (or clause) whose purpose is to take values for the variables **X** and **Y** and compute the sum of them using the statement **Z is X+Y.**

The variable names **X,Y,Z** are strictly local to the function definition which begins with the head **sum(X,Y,Z)** and ends at the full stop. The function is executed by using it's name and giving values, which are copied to the variables in the function definition (in Prolog it is said the variables **X** and **Y** are *instantiated* to their values).

Slight modifications may be made to give

sum(X,Y) :— Z is X+Y, nl, write(Z).

The body of the clause, which extends from **:—** to the full stop, contains three items separated by commas and these are executed from left to right.

?— sum(1,2).   User presses RETURN
                   A space line appears.

3 yes
?—   The answer is given, there is no
                   need to press RETURN.

Evidently the **nl** generated a new line of output and the **write** function displayed the value of **Z.**

Now take a rather different program which contains two (very short) clauses,

phone-number(brian, 2971).
phone-number(mike, 2854).

4

Execute this program,

```
?- phone-number(A,2971).
A= brian
yes
?- phone-number(mike,A).
A= 2854
yes
?- phone-number(jim,A).
no
?-
```

The behaviour above can be understood in terms of Prolog's pattern matching feature. A program statement of the kind **phone-number(brian, 2971)** is regarded as a true fact, so a query of the form **phone-number (A,2971)** can be made the same as the fact when **A** takes the value **brian**. More than one such fact may be included in a program. Where the query cannot match a fact the system returns the answer **no.**

The next program contains both of the types of clauses introduced up to this point:

```
working(x) :-employee(X).
employee(brian).
employee(ann).
employee(mike).
```

The program (which comprises the four clauses shown) may be given a query

```
?- working(ann).
yes
```

The Prolog interpreter tries to prove the goal **working(ann)** by using the rule which leads to a subgoal **employee(ann).** This is satisfied by one of the clauses in the program so the rule is true, and thus the query is true.

The next program (called **max**) combines all the types of clauses discussed up to this point:

```
/* This computes the max of two numbers */
max(X,X,X).
max(X,Y,Y) :- X<Y.
max(X,Y,X) :- Y<X.
```

The result of executing $X<Y$ is a boolean (true or false). It returns true only when the value of X is less than the value of Y. Executing the program,

```
?- max(1,2,Y).
Y=2
yes
?- max(25,1,Y).
Y=25
yes
?- max(5,5,Y).
Y=5
yes
```

The first result above is given by a matching with the second program clause, giving $X=1$, $Y=2$ and the boolean $X<Y$ as true. When a clause is true, Prolog does not seek alternatives but returns the appropriate values.

The last result derives from the fact **max(X,X,X).** with **X=5,** which is the only clause to be true with this query. Prolog seeks from the first clause which matches the query name, and works through each one trying to satisfy the query (make it true).

In one sense Prolog programming is designed to produce either of the two answers true or false (yes or no) only. However to do this it often has to match variables (like **Y** above) to values or other variables. These matchings, such as **Y=25,** are then available as results.

Obtaining answers in a Prolog program is very much a 'side effect' of the general activity which is

(1) make a general match with a head of a clause
(2) move to the body (right-hand side) of a clause and try to prove its parts true
(3) if the above fails, go back to (1) looking for another clause.

Consider the previous program in the light of the above comments,

```
?– max(X,2,3).
X=3
yes
?– max(1,X,4).
X=4
yes
```

The results are not what might be expected from a conventional programming language but are explained by the pattern matching, proving scheme of Prolog. Even the following works:

```
?— max(X,Y,4).
X=4,
Y=4
yes
```

Or a query containing all constants,

```
?— max(1,2,2).
yes
?— max(1,2,3).
no
```

User response to an answer

When the result of a query is **yes** or **no,** no further response is required, the system will prompt for the next input (by **?—** or similar).

When the result involves variables in the head of the clause taking values (being *instantiated*) then values are displayed. These may be accepted by pressing RETURN, the system responds **yes** and prompts as above. However, alternative matchings for the variables may be possible. To obtain these type **;** (read as OR). Any other values will be displayed or **no** if there are no others.

Running Prolog programs

Prolog is normally used as an interactive system, although compilers are also available. The latter are used for large developed programs to improve their execution speed.

Each computer system will have its own means of loading the Prolog interpreter.

Programs may be prepared using the usual utilities provided by the computer (e.g. the editor) and stored in files. When the Prolog interpreter has been started, the following predicates (which may be thought of as functions at this stage) may be used to load the program from a file.

consult(F)   **reconsult(F)**

consult(F) instructs the Prolog system to read the file **F, reconsult** acts like **consult** but replaces any clauses which have the same name as those already loaded. It is used normally to replace some existing clauses with modified versions on a test basis.

Examples

consult('PROG1.PRO').
reconsult('EXAMPLE.TXT').

A special form of consult and reconsult,

consult(user).   **reconsult(user).**

may be available. They allow clauses to be typed directly into the Prolog system from the users' terminal. Such input is terminated by using the CTRL and Z keys, or CTRL and D keys, together.

To examine the state of the program which has been loaded, two predicates are available,

listing(C)   **listing**

listing will list to the terminal all the clauses in the current program, **listing(C)** lists the clauses which have a name given by **C**.

Example

listing(sum).

lists all the clauses which are called **sum.**

Programs and Clauses

The fundamental idea behind Prolog is that a collection of logic statements can be regarded as a program. Execution is a suitably controlled logical deduction using the clauses forming the program. This process is often likened to theorem proving.

The logic statements in Prolog are restricted to one conclusion (the left-hand side, below) as a result of the computation on a set of conditions (the right-hand side, below).

Goal :– subgoal$_1$, subgoal$_2$, ... subgoal$_N$.

This logic statement may be read as,

'If subgoal$_1$ is true AND subgoal$_2$ is true AND ... AND subgoal$_N$ is true THEN Goal is true.'

This form of logic statement is known as a HORN clause. (Distinguished from general predicate logic statements by having only one Goal.)

Basic syntax

A Prolog program consists of a set of *procedures*.
Each procedure name is called a *predicate* because
its value may be true or false, only. A procedure may
contain one or more *clauses* (all of the same name).
Details of syntax to note are,

- the clauses are written out almost entirely using
  lower-case letters, because upper-case letters are
  reserved for variable names.
- round brackets are used to enclose the parameter
  lists of predicates.
- every clause is terminated by a full stop.

Here is an example program to convert the value of
money to dollars, marks, or francs from pounds.
Integer values are assumed. Some prolog systems do
not support real numbers.

```
money(francs, 11).
money(dollars, 2).
money(marks, Y) :— money(dollars, Rate),
                   Y is Rate * 2.
from_pounds(Number, Type) :—
    money(Type, Y), V is Number *Y,
    write (V) ,write(Type).
```

The program contains the two procedures **money**
and **from_pounds.** Money contains three clauses,
two of which are in a short form which is often
referred to as a 'fact'. The money procedure sets the
rate of exchange, giving the number of francs and
dollars to a pound. The third clause shows that the
exchange rate for the mark is twice the rate for the

dollar. The program may be used to convert from pounds to either dollars, francs or marks.

```
?– from_pounds(3, dollars)
6 dollars yes
?– from_pounds (20, francs).
220 francs yes
?– from_pounds(15, marks).
60 marks yes
```

Programs and clauses

Prolog programs are collections of clauses. All clauses take the general form,

head :– body

one predicate name
with, possibly, a
list of arguments in
brackets

one or more subgoals
separated by (**,**) or
possibly (**;**)

One special case is,

head.

interpreted as a fact (always true).

Another special case is,

:– body

one or more subgoals, as above,

it is usually written as,

?–body.

or

<–body.

In all cases it is interpreted as the goal(s) which the Prolog system seeks to establish.

In summary

- a clause head without a body is called a *fact* or *assertion*.
- a clause with both head and body is called a *rule*.
- a clause body without a head is called a *query*. A Prolog program is executed by giving it a query.

Terms

All the objects which appear in Prolog programs are called *terms*. They include clauses, predicates, goals, variables, atoms and compound terms.

An *atom* is made up from letters, digits and other symbols, normally beginning with a letter. An atom identifies the smallest individual part of a clause. Thus 'francs', 'dollars' and 'marks' in the above example are atoms. Atoms are constants.

Variables can have values attributed to them during the execution of a program. When a value is attributed to a variable it is said to be *instantiated*. This is rather stronger than the idea of assigning values to variables in other languages such as BASIC. Technically, if a variable is instantiated to a

13

value it has been given an instance of one of the possible members of the value class. For example, X being instantiated to 5 means that X has been given an instance of an integer, the one which is the number five.

In Prolog both the user and the system, during computation, may instantiate variables, but only the system may re-instantiate a variable, usually during searching or backtracking.

Anything which starts with an upper-case letter or the underline character is taken by the Prolog system to be a variable. Examples of variables are,

```
X   Y   Rate    Type    N21
_next   _BRIAN   _10    _2X
```

The underline character may be used to create readable predicate names such as **from_pounds.** It has a further important use in Prolog as an *anonymous variable*. Referring to the example program **max** on p.6, the goals below both succeed,

```
?– max(1,2,2).
yes
?– max (1,2,_).
yes
```

In the second case the last parameter to **max** was an anonymous variable. As a variable it would match any value, so the goal succeeds. When more than one anonymous variable is used in a clause, Prolog regards each occurrence as a distinct variable.

Two further points concerning variables:

- variables are not 'data typed' as in languages such as FORTRAN. A variable may be instantiated to any Prolog term.
- the scope of variables is limited to the clause in which they are defined. There are no global variables in Prolog.

A predicate describes a relationship between other terms. It may be true or false. The simplest predicate is a clause without a body, for example,

dog(gemma).

which is interpreted as a predicate that is always true. It is probably intended to be read as 'gemma is a dog'. Variables may be included,

dog(X).

which in this case is not very useful, since it is likely to mean 'any value X is a dog'.

More complex predicates depend upon the system proving subgoals to be true or false.

dog(X) :-barks(X), has_legs(4,X).

The above could be read as 'X is a dog if X barks and X has four legs'.

There are a range of *built-in predicates* provided by the system. For example,

atom(T)

returns true if term **T** is an atom. Most built-in predicates are provided not just because they return true or false but for the 'side effects' they produce. For example,

write(T)

usually returns true, while writing the term **T** to the terminal or a file. The side-effects of these predicates give many of the features required to make Prolog a general purpose programming language.

Constants refer to specific objects or specific relationships. Constants include atoms, integers, real numbers, strings. For example,

0   514   −23   are integers (some systems use ~ to indicate negative values)

"Brian"   "An actor and his Time"
are strings

Anything between double quotes is treated as a string. There is a direct equivalence between a string and its internal representation by Prolog as a list of its character codes (usually ASCII). Using list manipulation, strings may be easily taken apart and changed.

Program layout

In general, a program will contain a set of procedures. Some procedures may contain facts and rules, others may contain either just rules or just facts.

The order in which program clauses are set out may be very important for its correct execution. Details are given in the next section on p.19.

A typical layout is

```
rule.
            a set of procedures
fact.
rule


fact.
fact.       sometimes referred
   .        to as the 'Database'
   .

   .
fact.
```

The following program is an example of this layout:

```
/* Program to find descendants */
has_descendant(X,Z) :-mother(X,Z).
has_descendant(X,Y) :-mother(X,A),
   has_descendant(A,Y).
mother(jane, mark).
mother(jane, paula).
mother(paula, tom).
is_aged(jane, 45).
is_aged(mark, 23).
is_aged(paula, 25).
is_aged(tom, 3).
```

The program is executed with a number of goals, firstly,

?–has_descendant (jane, Child).
Child = **mark** ;
Child = **paula** ;
Child = **tom;**
no

This is a simple goal. Request all the answers by typing **;** after each answer.

There are no more alternatives

The first two answers used the first clause of the procedure **has_descendant** and matched the subgoal **mother** immediately with a fact. The third answer used the second clause of **has_descendant** to produce paula, and examined her children by using the first clause. Notice the recursive feature of this procedure, which is very common in Prolog programs. Continuing with another goal,

?–has_descendant(jane, Child), is_aged (**Child, N**).
Child = **mark, N**=**23** ;
Child = **paula, N**=**25** ;
Child = **tom, N**=**3;**

This is a more complex goal. Note the comma between predicates which means AND. Request all answers.

no

Complex goals may be constructed. Here is one to find two descendants of jane's whose ages differ by exactly 20 years.

```
?–has_descendant(jane, X), is_aged(X,N),
    has_descendant(jane, Y), is_aged(Y,M),
      M=:=N+20.
X=tom, N=3, Y=mark, M=23 ;
no
```

The final clause **M=:=N** tests for equality between the values instantiated with **M** and **N.**

How Prolog Programs work

The semantics of Prolog are essentially those of resolution logic. But resolution logic itself does not constitute a programming language. Statements in resolution logic are descriptive. They have the form 'X is true'. In conventional programming languages the statements are imperative. They have the form 'perform action X'. To derive a programming language from resolution logic it is necessary to add imperative statements of the form 'prove that X is true'. A statement of this form is called a goal statement.

The language now allows us to request the construction of a proof. But how will the attempt at a proof proceed? The proof procedure for Prolog uses resolution in a simple depth-first, left-to-right search strategy. This proof procedure is not complete. Because of the depth-first strategy a proof may not be found even if one exists in the search space. The proof procedure may follow an infinite branch in the search tree and never examine another branch which could yield a satisfactory proof. However, if the proof procedure terminates we know that it has found the right answer. If it terminates with success then a proof exists. If it terminates with failure then no proof exists in the search space.

This simple search strategy may seem unsatisfactory since it yields an incomplete proof procedure, but it has numerous advantages over more general strategies. It can be implemented in a manner which is more efficient in the use of space than current breadth-first search methods. The simplicity of the Prolog search strategy makes it easy for the programmer to understand and control the search. The strict ordering of the search permits the use of built-in predicates causing side-effects (e.g. **read** and **write**) with the knowledge that the side-effects will occur in a prescribed order. The prospect of output being created in random order does not seem very pleasant! Thus, it is evident that the simple search strategy possesses several desirable characteristics.

User predicates

The meanings assigned to user-defined predicates
are entirely a matter for the user. Prolog sees
predicates only as patterns of symbols to be matched
against similar patterns during execution. The
constraint on the user is to keep the meanings
consistent throughout the program.

For example,

likes (brian, sheila).

could mean 'brian likes sheila' or 'sheila likes brian'
which are quite different interpretations. It is a matter
for the user (or brian and sheila) to decide which one
is desired and program accordingly.

Of course, a suitable choice of predicate names
can help to indicate the interpretation, as can the
atoms involved as parameters,

likes (colin, cars)

seems to have the natural meaning 'colin likes cars'.

Operators are available (*see* the section on
operators, p.76) which can be user-defined to make
a program more readable, so that,

sheila likes jo.

could be a valid clause using a specially defined
operator **likes.**

Clauses

Clauses can be understood from two points of view. Firstly, they can be understood in terms of the predicate logic which underlies Prolog. That is, they are identified as universally quantified implications, with the quantification applying to all the variables in the clause. For example,

**descendant (X,Z) :–offspring (X,Y),
descendant (Y,Z).**

may be read as

'for all X, Y, Z
Z is a descendant of X if Y is one of the offspring of X and Z is a descendant of Y.'

In clauses and terms all variables are assumed to be universally quantified. That is, a clause or term containing variables is valid for any values which the variables may take.

Secondly, clauses may be understood as pieces of a program. Since a procedure may contain more than one clause, each clause corresponds to a 'case' of the procedure.

Each of the cases will be tried in turn to establish the truth of the procedure. When this has been proved the procedure exits. The above clause, in this view, may be interpreted as

'to find a Z that is a descendant of X, find a Y that is the offspring of X, and then find a Z that is a descendant of Y.'

Prolog execution

Prolog execution is started by a goal statement. A goal statement is a request for a proof. The execution of a Prolog program is essentially the action of an elementary theorem prover attempting a proof.

To execute such a goal the Prolog system matches it against the head of each clause in turn until it finds a match with the predicate name having the same number of arguments as the goal. In seeking a match Prolog always tries the clauses in the order they appear in the program (from beginning to end). Having found a matching head, Prolog looks at the body (if any) of the clause and proceeds with each subgoal in left-to-right order.

The matching process, known as *unification,* succeeds if the goal and clause head can be made identical by 'filling in' suitable values for the variables.

If for some reason one of the subgoals is found to be false, then the Prolog system will go back to the previous subgoal (to the left) and attempt to re-evaluate it using different facts and rules in the program. If this attempt succeeds the goal on the right (which initially failed) is evaluated again, but possibly with different values for its variables. Again if this fails an attempt will be made to re-evaluate the subgoal on the left. This process is known as *backtracking.* As subgoals are being evaluated in the body of a clause the Prolog system keeps an individual marker in the program for each subgoal as it is satisfied (found true). Backtracking causes a search from each marker towards the end of the program. When the end is reached the subgoal cannot be re-evaluated and backtracking proceeds with the next leftmost subgoal, or the whole clause fails if there are no more subgoals.

Unification

Unification is a generalised form of substitution for variables. A substitution replaces all occurrences of a variable by a term. The replacing term may be a constant (such as **abc** or **32**), a structure (such as **f(a)** or **g(x,y)**) or another variable. For example, if we substitute **a** for **x** in **g(x,f(x))** then the resulting term is **g(a,f(a))**. If we substitute **f(y)** for **x** in **h(x,y)** then the result is **h(f(y),y)**.

When one or more substitutions are applied to a term, the result is an instance of the term. For example,

son(fred,colin) :—father(colin, fred).

is an instance of

son(X,Y) :—father(Y,X).

A Prolog proof

A series of diagrams may be used to describe the progress of a Prolog proof. Each diagram, called an *implication tree,* describes the state of the proof at a given point in time. An implication tree consists of

one or more labelled nodes. At the top of the
diagram is a node labelled 'goal'. Each of the other
nodes is labelled with a predicate and is joined to a
parent node immediately above it.

When the predicate labelling the node has been
proven the node is marked with a P.

To illustrate the proof process which contains both
unification and backtracking, consider the following
example:

son(X,Y) :–father(Y,X).
father(john, fred).
father(john, george).
father(al, bert).
father(george, al).

It is desired to prove the goal,

?– son(Z, john).

By 'proving a goal' is meant finding an instance of
the goal which Prolog can prove. In this case the
generation of the solution, **Z=fred,** will be traced.
The proof is illustrated using implication trees. The
initial tree is

goal
|
son(Z, john)

Now Prolog seeks an instance of a clause which can
be used in the proof of

son(Z, john).

The appropriate instance is formed from

son(X,Y) :–father(Y,X)

by substituting **Z** for **X** and **john** for **Y** to give

son(Z, john) :–father(john, Z).

The tree now is

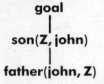

Note that Prolog found substitutions that made the head of a clause the same as the current subterm. The general process of finding substitutions to make two terms the same is called *unification*. Next, Prolog seeks to find a clause whose head will unify with **father(john, Z).** The first clause for **father** matches if **fred** is substituted for **Z.** This gives the completed implication tree,

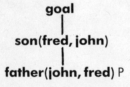

and the result **Z=fred** is generated.

Backtracking (described fully on p.52) is shown in following the proof process using a more complex goal clause,

?–father(john, X), father(X,Y).

The proof proceeds as follows:

goal

father(john, X)   **father(X,Y)**

X is instantiated to **fred**

goal

P **father(john,fred)**   **father(fred, Y)**

The attempt to solve the subgoal **father(fred, Y)**
fails since this term will not unify with any of the
clause heads. Backtracking occurs and the proof is
backed up to the point where the
father(john,fred) clause was activated. This
clause is then deactivated and any substitutions
made when (or since) this clause was selected are
undone. This restores the proof to the point,

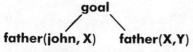

goal

father(john, X)   **father(X,Y)**

The clause **father(john, george)** is about to be
selected for unification with **father(john, X)**. This
unification succeeds giving,

goal

P **father(john, george)**   **father(george, Y)**

The clauses for **father** are then selected in turn for
unification with **father(george, Y).** The unification

succeeds for the clause **father(george, al)**, yielding the completed implication tree.

goal

P **father(john, george)**   **father(george, al)** P

Thus producing **X=george, Y=al,** as one solution.

Control of execution

Controlling the path of clause execution in a Prolog program depends on the following:

- the ordering of clauses within the program, because Prolog always scans from beginning to end.
- the ordering of subgoals; the body of a clause. Execution is always left to right.
- backtracking occurs automatically when a subgoal, or clause in the body of another fails. It proceeds right to left.
- there are other features which can be used to control execution, these include the cut (*see* p.56) and recursion (*see* p.44)

Arithmetic and Equality Predicates

Since Prolog is designed for logic and symbolic programming the inclusion of arithmetic facilities is essentially secondary. Some Prolog systems restrict numeric values to integer type.

The equivalent of 'assigning a value' to a variable is to instantiate it using the **is** predicate, thus,

X is Y

causes the variable, or expression, **Y** to be evaluated and the result instantiated with **X.** The result is always true, provided a syntax error is not made in **X** or **Y.**
Remember, because it is a functional language Prolog allows only *one* instantiation of a variable per clause,

does_not_work(X) :–X is 1, write(X), X is X+1, write(X).

The clause would fail on the third subgoal **X is X**+**1.**

Operations

A set of standard arithmetic operators is available for use in expressions on the right-hand side of the **is** predicate,

Y+**Z**	addition
Y–**Z**	subtraction
Y*Z**	multiplication
Y/Z	division
Y mod Z	remainder of Y divided by Z

The + and – operators have a higher priority than the *, **/** and **mod** operators. (*See* the section on Operators, p.76, for a discussion.) A negation operator may use a standard minus sign or a system dependent symbol such as ~ (tilde).

–**X**	negation (unary minus)

29

The arithmetic operators are defined to be left-associative, which means that operators with equal priority are evaluated from left to right,

1 + 10 + 12 is evaluated as (1 + 10) + 12
10/5/2 is evaluated as (10/5)/2

and

12 + 13/4/2 is evaluated as 12 + ((13/4)/2)

The values of variables and expressions may be tested with a range of predicates which return true if the condition is satisfied.

Y=:=Z **Y** and **Z** are evaluated, true if results are equal

Y\=Z true if **Y** and **Z** evaluate to different values

Y<Z true if the value of **Y** is less than the value of **Z**

Y>Z true if the value of **Y** is greater than the value of **Z**

Y=<Z true if the value of **Y** is less than or equal to the value of **Z**

Y>=Z true if the value of **Y** is greater than or equal to the value of **Z**

Systems vary in their implementation of the last two predicates which may be available as <= and =>, respectively.

The following examples show the application of
arithmetic features (integer values are assumed):

```
/* calculates the absolute value of X */
abs(X,X) :-X >= 0.
abs(X,Y) :-Y is ~ X.

/* tests whether X is even */
even(X) :-Z is X mod 2, Z=:=0.

/* calculates X raised to the power of Y*/
/* and gives the result in Z */
exp(X,0,1).
exp(X,Y,Z) :-A is Y - 1, exp(X,A,B), Z is
   B*X.
```

The procedure **exp** is recursive following the rule
that,

$$X^Y = X^{Y-1} \cdot X$$

but with the termination condition $X^0 = 1$, as long as Y
is a positive integer.

Equality

Core Prolog provides several types of test for
equality between terms.

X=:=Y   arithmetic

X and **Y** are arithmetic expressions and are first
evaluated to produce (perhaps integer) values. Then
the results are tested for equality.

If **Z** is *already* instantiated to a value, the predicate

Z is X   arithmetic

will evaluate **X,** and the result will be true if it has the same value as **Z.**

A general test for equality is given by

X=**Y**   general test

Full matching is applied to **X** and **Y** to try and make them the same. If there is a match the goal succeeds. In particular, uninstantiated variables will match anything.

A very strict test for equality which succeeds only when **X** and **Y** are literally identical is

X==**Y**   strict test

The test is one for the same identity of the item on either side of the predicate.

The == predicate will not succeed with matching two uninstantiated variables, unless they are the same object. (They can be made the same by a previous matching.)

When the == test succeeds between two items, then the = test will also succeed, but the converse is not necessarily true.

Predicates testing for non-equality corresponding to the above types are available,

X=\=**Y**   arithmetic
X\=**Y**   general
X\==**Y**   strict

Input and Output Predicates

This section deals with predicates which programs may use to read and write information to/from the user's terminal and to/from files.

The predicates generally succeed when used for information transfer, unless some serious input/output error occurs. They succeed only once, and cannot be re-satisfied during backtracking.

Input predicates can be used to test a preset value against the items to be read next, and thus operate in a logical manner. However, information transfer (like arithmetic) is a 'side-effect' as far as logic programming is concerned.

Input

read (X)

A term (*see* p.13) is read from the current input source (user or file) and instantiated with **X.** The term must be syntactically correct and is terminated by a full stop which is not transmitted to **X.** The full stop must be followed by a non-printing character, such as a space or carriage return.

In Table 1 the predicate **read(X)** was used to read the terms given in the left-hand column, and the result which was instantiated with **X** is given in the right-hand column.

Table 1

Term as input	**X** is instantiated to
1.	**1**
word.	**word**
Variable.	**_20**
pred(a,b,C).	**pred(a,b,_13)**
ok :–C is 4*5, write (C).	**ok :–_11 is 4*5, write(_11)**
[A, a, B, b].	**[_15, a, _16, b]**
'brian'.	**brian**
"brian".	**[98, 114, 105, 97, 110]**

Note that variables (which start with a capital letter) are represented in their internal form, which is the underline character followed by a number.

Single quotes allow the symbols contained to be passed unaltered to **X,** effectively turning off the syntax check.

Double quotes cause the string to be represented as a list of character codes. In the example, ASCII codes are shown.

get0(X)   get(X)

Both predicates read a single character from the input source, and **X** is instantiated with this character code. **get** skips over (ignores) spaces, and all non-printing characters.

Example
Load the clause

```
next :–get(X), tab(12), write(X).
?– next.
1                                   press return, no full stop
        49 yes
?–
```

In the above, 49 is the ASCII code for the character 1.

skip(N)

Characters are read from the current input source
until a character with code **N** is encountered.

Example
Load the clause

```
more :–get(X), skip(53), write (X).
?– more.
1
5                                   press return for each line
49 yes
?
```

The clause **skip(53)** reads characters and waits
until one with an ASCII code 53 is input. This code is
the character 5. The value of output given by **more**
was the first character read before the **skip,** the
number 1 with ASCII code 49.

Output

write(X)	**writeq(X)**
print(X)	**display(X)**

The term **X** is written to the output destination. **write** uses any operator declarations to format the result, **display** ignores operator declarations. **writeq** puts single quotes round unusual characters, so that its output may be read using **read(X). print(X)** is similar to **write(X),** but system dependent.

Table 2 shows the effect of writing various terms, instantiated with **X,** using three output predicates.

Table 2

X is instantiated to	write(X)	writeq(X)	display(X)
atom	atom	atom	atom
_4	_4	_4	_4
'OK'	OK	'OK'	'OK'
[a,b,C]	[a,b,_15]	[a,b,_15]	.'(a,.'(b,.'(_15,[])))
C is 4*5	_11 is 4*5	_11 is 4*5	is(_11,*(4,5))

When **display** is used a prefix notation is printed out with operators printed before the arguments.

put(N)

The character with code **N** is written to the output destination.

tab(N)   nl

tab(N) causes **N** spaces to be written to the output, an **nl** causes a new line to be started.

Examples

put(98)	will generate the output character 6
	(assuming ASCII codes)
tab(6)	will generate six spaces to the output

Testing input

Both **read(X)** and **get(X)** can be used with **X** instantiated, to test the values next encountered on the input source. In addition, with **read(X)** at the end of file, **X** is instantiated to 'end-of-file' and **get0(X)** is instantiated to the end of file character.

Input example

Unlike input using non-AI languages the **read(X)** does not just read 'lumps' of data, it also checks that they conform to Prolog syntax as complete terms. This can sometimes work against what the programmer requires. In such a case another procedure may be constructed using the basic read

predicate **get0.** The example shows a procedure
get_letters(Z) which reads in a set of characters
until a space character is encountered. The result is a
list of the character codes instantiated with **Z**.

```
get_letters([X|Y]) :–get0(X), X\=32,
                      get_letters(Y).
get_letters([ ]).
```
when executed,
```
?– get_letters(Z).
```
brian

   a space is typed after the n, return is pressed

Z = [98,114,105,97,110].

This compares with the string input example in the
section on input, p.35, but no quotes or a full stop are
required. In general terms **get_letters** reads a
character, checks that it is not equal to a space
(ASCII code 32), then calls itself to get the next
character. When the first clause fails because **X** is a
space, backtracking cannot cause **get0** to be
reactivated (as it succeeds only once), so the second
clause is tried and succeeds with an empty list value.
Recursion unwinds itself building up the full list as the
value instantiated to **Z.** For further details of
recursion *see* p.44.

Output examples

Recursive procedures are used to obtain an item, send it to the output and try to obtain the next item. When there are no more items left, the procedure uses an alternative clause to output a newline. Here are two examples, **write_line** and **put_line**:

```
write_line([ ]) :-nl.
write_line(X|Y) :-write(X), tab(1),
                   write_line(Y).

put_line([ ]) :-nl.
put_line([X|Y]) :-put(X), put_line(Y).
```

These are executed as

```
?-write_line(['Have', 'a', 'good', 'day',
              'Sheila!']).
Have a good day Sheila!
?-put_line("Have a good day Sheila!").
Have a good day Sheila!
```

The items manipulated by the two procedures are quite different. **write_line** handles atoms from a list, whereas **put_line** handles individual characters. Recall that a string with double quotes is treated as a list of character codes.

Not all the atoms in the **write_line** example need to be enclosed in quotes; only those which contain strange symbols, or begin with a capital letter (and thus would otherwise be taken as a variable).

File handling

Terms and characters may be transmitted between program and files using the predicates described earlier in this section.

The destination of input and output is the user terminal by default, until changed by specifying a file using **tell(F)** and **see(F).**

see(F)   seeing(F)

see(F) selects **F** to be the current input file, and opens it for input. **seeing(F)** finds the name of the current input source and instantiates **F** with this name.

seen

seen closes the current input file and sets input back to the terminal.

tell(F)   telling(F)

tell(F) selects **F** to be the current output file and opens it for output. **telling(F)** finds the name of the current output and instantiates **F** with this name.

told   close(F)

told closes the current output file and sets output back to the terminal. **close(F)** closes the file **F.**

The duration of file connection is limited to the dynamic scope of the clause which contains the file opening and closing predicates. That is, any clauses invoked from this clause may direct I/O to the selected file. Leaving a file open by failing the clause which opened it usually closes the file, but may result in any input or output which was in a buffer area being lost.

Provided the computer operating system allows it, it is possible to have several files open simultaneously, but note the example details,

```
....  tell(A), write('to file A'), nl, tell(B),
      write('to file B'), tell (A), write('A
      again'), told.
```

generates in the file whose name is instantiated to A,

to file A
A again

and to the other file,

to file B

The following example is an attempt to redefine the top-level actions of the Prolog interpreter so that a record of the interactive work is sent to a file, and displayed to the user in the usual way.

The procedure **goal** opens the file which is to receive the results during the interactive session,

```
goal :–nl, write ('Please give the output
       file name :–'),
       read(X), tell(X), continue(X), told.
```

The **continue()** procedure will repeatedly read a term, evaluate it and send the result to the output file. Much of **continue()** consists of **write** procedures which give a nice user interface, if these are ignored for a moment, it is

```
continue(F) :– repeat, read(X), (X=stop ;
call(X), write(X), fail).
```

Within the brackets in the body of the clause is the semicolon meaning OR. The brackets will succeed if **X=stop** is true, or **call(X)**, **write(X)**, **fail** is true. The read instantiates **X** to a term, if **X** is not equal to **stop** then **X** is evaluated using **call** and written to the file. Next the **fail** is reached. Backtracking begins and goes immediately back to the beginning (left-hand end) of the body because the predicates **read, write** cannot be re-satisfied. **repeat** does nothing, it is always true, but can be re-satisfied during backtracking. Thus the forward testing begins again with **read(X)**.

A fuller version of **continue()** is

```
continue(F) :—repeat, tell(user), write(':—'),
             tell (F),
             read(X), (X=stop ; nl, nl,
                 write([':—',X]),
             nl, call(X), write(X), nl,
                 tell(user), write('**'),
             write(X), nl, write('YES'),
                 nl, nl, fail).
```

It is executed by asking for **goal** to be proved and the user sees

```
?- goal.
Please give the output file name :-
  'Record.dat;'.
:-assert(brian(ok)).
** assert(brian (ok))
YES
:-brian(X).
** brian(ok)
YES
:-stop.
yes
?-
```

the file record also contains goals and results as
follows:

```
[:-,assert(brian(ok))]
assert(brian(ok))
[:-, brian(_9)]
brian(ok)
```

Controlling Execution of Programs

Detailed control of execution in a Prolog program
depends on three features,

- recursion
- procedure and clause ordering
- backtracking and the cut

Prolog is not wholly a declarative language. Unfortunately, a detailed knowledge of the execution path in a program is often necessary to design it to obtain the correct results. However, such an execution path may be very complicated if all three features above are used too liberally in a large program.

Recursion

Recursion is a familiar feature in a number of procedural languages. It is the process in which a procedure (or clause) contains a call to itself. The calls to itself must cease at some point or the program will never terminate. Each recursive procedure must contain a means of choosing an alternative within its body which does not call itself. In procedural languages this choice is an IF statement, whereas in Prolog it is usually an alternative clause which is involved when the main clause fails.

The example below is a procedure that calculates the factorial of a number. **N** is the number of which the result **R** is the factorial. The call **fac(N,R)** contains a call to itself with **fac(M,S).**

```
fac(0,1).
fac(N,R) :—M is N−1, fac(M,S), R is N*S.
```

The first clause **fac(0,1)** is the termination condition used when a call to **fac(M,S)** generates a value of 0 instantiated with **M.** Coming before the main clause of the procedure it is always tested first by the system

44

when seeking a **fac(0,S)** match.

Separate clauses in a procedure are to be read as if they are alternatives, and thus provide the choice necessary to halt the recursion.

The example may be re-written using the semicolon as OR, giving an explicit alternative within a clause,

fac(N,R) :– M is N – 1, (M=0, S is 1 ; fac(M,S)), R is N*S.

Recursion may be visualised by considering a simple metaphor. Imagine you are standing at the top of a flight of stairs and each step represents a state of a particular procedure call, say, **fac(M,S)**. Assume the goal **fac(3,X)** is given. The procedure is first called with **N**=3 and **X**=**R** (unknown), so write these values down on a piece of paper and leave it at the top of the stairs. Step down one stair when next **fac()** is called within itself. The values to this call are **M**=**N**=**2** and **S**=**R**. Write these values on a piece of paper and leave it on the step. Continue moving down the stairs leaving pieces of paper with the details of each call on them. Finally **fac(0,1)** is reached and recursion ceases. The system now 'unwinds' the calls which have been generated. This corresponds to climbing back up the stairs, picking up the pieces of paper and using the values on them in any further calculations.

Note: since each subgoal within the clause body is a predicate it may fail and cause backtracking. This can occur during both the recursive descent, and during the 'unwinding' ascent. Both circumstances can generate complex execution paths (*see p.52*).

The next example produces the same factorial calculation with the recursive call at the end of the clause, essentially meaning that it cannot fail during the ascent.

```
fac(N,R) :-fact(N, 1, R).
fact(0,X,X).
fact(N,X,R) :-M is N-1, Y is X*N,
                fact(M,Y,R).
```

Recursion may be generated by indirect means. The procedure **ok** is involved in such indirect recursion.

```
ok :- one, two.
one.
two :- three, ok.
three.
```

Program layout

The order of execution of the parts of a Prolog program are as follows:

(1) Within a program the clauses are always examined from the beginning of the program. If a match to a clause is found and the clause succeeds (is found to be true) then a marker is positioned at that clause. If a further search is initiated, either for additional solutions or because of failure, the search resumes, from the marker towards the end of the program.

(2) Within the body of a clause the search and subgoal testing proceeds from left to right.
(3) Backtracking within the body of a clause proceeds from right to left.

Figure 1 illustrates the execution paths defined above.

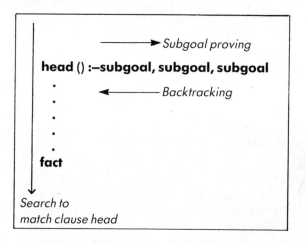

Figure 1 Schematic layout of a Prolog program

Clauses, the heads of which do not appear in the subgoals of other clauses, are the highest level of procedures in the program. They could be considered as the 'main program' parts in the other procedural languages. Clauses whose heads are subgoals of the highest level procedures may be said to be 'first level' clauses. Thus the program is logically a tree structure of clauses. A goal search need not always start with a clause at the top of the tree. Any clause may be queried. During the execution process it will use the clauses below it in the tree.

Programs are constructed using distinct items.
- Clauses which are always true (i.e. facts) and thus only consist of a head.
- Procedures which consist of one or more clauses, some of which may be of the form given above and are regarded as termination conditions.

How should these items be arranged?

Within a procedure the ordering of clauses may be crucial to its correct functioning. For example, the first factorial procedure given on p.44 will not work if it is written as

fac(N,R) :−M is N−1, fac(M,S), R is N + S.
fac(0,1).

because each recursive call will start looking for a match with **fac(N,R)** and this will always succeed since **N** and **R** are variables. The recursion will not stop until a system error like 'out of space' occurs.

The ordering of facts and procedures within a program does not affect the validity of the results, but may be a question of style and could affect efficiency.

It is generally useful to group the facts together as an easily located 'database'. The first example illustrates one popular layout,

```prolog
furry(sheba).
small_domestic_pet(sheba).
warm(sheba).
well_fed(sheba).
happy(X) :-purrs(X), cat(X).
purrs(X) :-well_fed(X), warm(X).
cat(X) :-furry(X), small_domestic_pet(X).
```

The layout is easily read by the programmer and the procedure clauses are arranged in the order of their 'levels'. The system when searching for subgoals, such as **cat(sheba)** will begin with the database and find the cat procedure after testing most of the heads of clauses in the program. However, most Prolog implementations use some type of indexing in the process of matching a subgoal to clause heads. The position of the clause in the program is, therefore, not, significant from an efficiency point of view.

A good layout is to position the procedures before the database, for microcomputer-based Prologs there may be an efficiency gain in allowing the system to find the subgoal clause heads near the beginning of each search of the program,

```prolog
happy(X) :-purrs(X), cat(X).
purrs(X) :-well_fed(X), warm(X).
cat(X) :-furry(X), small_domestic_pet(X).
furry(sheba).
small_domestic_pet(sheba).
warm(sheba).
well_fed(sheba).
```

Assert and retract

Several built-in predicates allow clauses to be added or removed from the program. They may be used by the programmer during interactive working, or by the program itself to modify its database or procedures.

assert(X)   **asserta(X)**   **assertz(X)**

The three predicates above add the new clause given by **X** to the program. **X** must be instantiated to a non-variable term, which is interpreted as a clause. **asserta** puts the clause as the first clause in the program and **assertz** puts it as the last clause. The position of the clause using **assert** is system dependent.

The actions of the **assert** predicates are not undone when backtracking occurs.

Examples of use

asserta(furry(tom)).

puts **furry(tom)** as first clause.

assertz((happy(X) :–purrs(X), cat(X))).

puts **happy(X) :–purrs(X), cat(X)** as last clause. Clauses may be removed from the program using the predicates,

retract(X)   **retractall(P)**

retract removes the first clause in the program which matches the clause instantiated to **X.** On backtracking it removes the next clause that matches

X. retractall removes all the clauses whose head matches **P**.

Examples

retractall(brian(_)).

will remove all clauses which are called **brian** and have one argument.

retract((out(_) :—nl, nl, write(_))).

will remove the specific clause

out(_) :—nl, nl, write(_).

The following example uses both **retract** and **assertz** to modify the fact **total (49)**, which exists in the database. Firstly **X** is instantiated with 49 then **total(49)** is retracted and the new fact asserted.

add_one :—retract(total(X)), Y is X+1,
**   assertz(total(Y)).**

    .
    .
    .
    .
    .

total(49).

The result of executing the goal add_one is to replace the fact **total (49)** with **total (50)**.

Backtracking

The structure of a Prolog clause may be schematically described as,

Goal :–subgoal$_1$, subgoal$_2$, ..., subgoal$_N$.

It is not possible to test and satisfy each subgoal simultaneously so the Prolog system proceeds from left to right. If for some reason one of the subgoals is found to be false then Prolog will go back to the previous subgoal on the left and attempt to re-evaluate it using the remaining clauses in the program. If this attempt fails then the next subgoal to the left is re-evaluated. This is *backtracking*.

Some built-in predicates cannot be re-satisfied during the backtracking. For example, **read** and **write.**

The following program illustrates the execution path of a simple program during backtracking. The graphical notation used in the section on Prolog proof on p.24 is used to demonstrate the state of the search. The theme of the example is taken from Jane Austen's *Pride and Prejudice*;

"It is a truth universally acknowledged that a single man in possession of a good fortune, must be in want of a wife."

```
who_marries_whom :-female(X), male(Y),
   rich(Y), write([X, 'marries', Y]),fail.
female(elizabeth).
female(jane).
male(collins).
male(darcy).
male(bingley).
rich(darcy).
rich(bingley).
?-who_marries_whom.
```

The goal is **who_marries_whom** and the first
subgoal is evaluated and proved (shown by letter P
below).

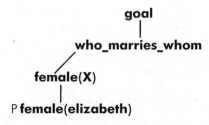

Similarly for the **male()** subgoal, which makes the
next subgoal become **rich(collins)** since **Y** is
instantiated to **collins**.

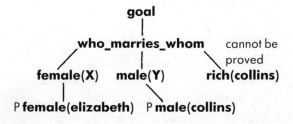

rich(collins) is false, so backtracking begins and
returns to **male(Y)**, which next instantiates **Y** to
darcy.

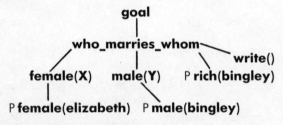

rich(darcy) is true, the **write** statement produces,

elizabeth marries darcy

fail is a predicate which is always false and causes
backtracking. **rich(darcy)** cannot be satisfied
again so back to **male(Y)** for re-evaluation.

goal

who_marries_whom
write()
female(X)   **male(Y)**   P **rich(bingley)**

P **female(elizabeth)**   P **male(bingley)**

Y is instantiated to **bingley** and all succeeds to
produce

elizabeth marries bingley

Evidently the results depart from the plot of the novel.
But at least Elizabeth does not marry Mr Collins.

Again, **fail** causes backtracking. This goes back to
female(X) since **male(Y)** cannot be re-satisfied as

54

there are no more **male()** facts left to match.

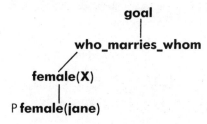

Evaluation proceeds to the right to give

Backtracking produces a solution as far as the write predicate,

goal
|
who_marries_whom ——— **write()**
/ | \
female(X)   **male(Y)**   P **rich(darcy)**
| |
P **female(jane)**   P **male(darcy)**

causing the result

jane marries darcy

55

The **fail** and consequent backtracking produce a multiple set of solutions which permutes elizabeth and jane as marrying darcy and bingley. Can anything be done to control all this backtracking?

The answer lies in the predicate called the *cut* which is represented by an exclamation mark (**!**). Logically it is a predicate without any arguments which is always true. As a subgoal it succeeds but cannot be re-satisfied. Once it has been passed through (from left to right), it cannot be passed through in the other direction (the one which backtracking follows). So it acts as a sort of valve.

Using the cut means that when the subgoal immediately to the right of it fails, then since backtracking cannot go past it, the whole clause must fail.

Consider the introduction of the cut to the left of **fail** in the previous example.

```
who_marries_whom :-female(X), male(Y),
                    rich(Y),
                    write([X, 'marries',
                    Y]), !, fail.
female(elizabeth).
           .
           .
           .

rich(bingley).
```

Execution proceeds exactly as in the first three diagrams of this example previously. This includes backtracking over Mr Collins, before both the **write()** and **!** (the cut) are reached. A solution is produced,

elizabeth marries darcy

Next the *cut* is reached and succeeds. **fail** tries to cause backtracking which is now prevented by the cut. The whole clause fails and execution stops leaving the single solution above.

Placing the cut earlier in the clause,

who_marries_whom :—female(X), !,
male(Y), rich(Y),
write ([X, 'marries',
Y]), fail.

together with the same database will allow backtracking amongst the rich males (don't these people always have a good time), but restrict the solution to one female, giving

elizabeth marries darcy.

and

elizabeth marries bingley.

With this simple program, even using the cut, it is not possible to get the unique solution given in the novel that elizabeth marries darcy, and jane marries bingley.

The following example illustrates the effect of backtracking and the *cut* when several procedures are nested. The program does not do anything useful, each clause writes out a message to allow the execution path to be followed.

```
pred1(A) :–write('body of 1'), pred2(A).
pred2(A) :–write('body of 2'), pred3,
            pred4(A).
pred2(A) :–nl, write('again in 2, does not
            call pred3 and pred4 this
            time').
pred3 :–write('body of 3').
pred3 :–nl, write('again in 3').
pred4(A) :–write('body of 4, A='),write(A),
            !, A:=2.
pred4(A) :–write('again in 4, A='),write(A).
```

The test after the *cut* in **pred4** succeeds only when **A** is instantiated to **2.** Here are the results in that case.

```
?– pred1(2).
body of 1   body of 2   body of 3   body of
   4, A=2
yes
```

Several backtracking cycles take place when **A** is not instantiated to **2.**

The results are,

```
?– pred1(3).
body of 1   body of 2   body of 3   body of
   4, A=3
again in 3   body of 4, A=3
again in 2, does not call pred3 and pred4
   this time
yes
```

One point to note: when the test following the *cut* in
pred4 fails the whole procedure fails because of
the *cut*. The second clause of **pred4** is never
accessed, either because the test in the first clause is
successful and it is not required or because of failure
and the *cut*.

The diagrams below follow the progress of the goal
pred1(3).

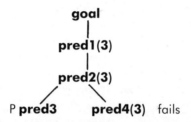

The first line of output has been produced at this
stage. Backtracking causes the second clause of
pred3 to be tried (from **pred2**).

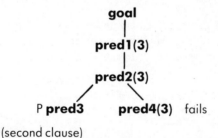

(second clause)

The second line of output has been produced at this
stage. Backtracking means that the second clause of
pred2 is tried (from **pred1**).

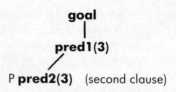

goal

pred1(3)

P **pred2(3)**   (second clause)

This succeeds as **pred4** is not called, and the final line of output is produced.

In summary, backtracking may be controlled using the *cut*. There are three main uses of the *cut*.

- The programmer expects the clause to succeed and wants to indicate to the system that it has found the right choice of clause for a particular goal, and does not wish the system to pick any other clauses if the clause fails.
- The programmer wants the system to fail in a particular clause immediately without trying other solutions. Perhaps because an error condition is expected. The conjunction

  !,fail.

  is used.
- The program succeeds with solutions but the programmer wishes to prevent the generation of alternative solutions and so inserts a cut.

Finally, there are a couple of useful predicates to be considered when backtracking is expected.

true   repeat

true always succeeds, but is not re-satisfied during backtracking. However, **repeat** always succeeds and is always re-satisfied during backtracking, which means it stops backtracking and starts forward goal proving again. See the next section for an example using **repeat.**

Iteration and alternation

The principle control structures in procedural languages are iteration (looping) and alternation (IF THEN ELSE). It is sometimes useful to mimic these constructs, provided the programmer is not trying to duplicate procedural programming in Prolog.

Clauses may be constructed to provide both the actions mentioned above, but they must not be taken as direct equivalents to the procedural constructs they mimic.

The predicate below is called as **loop(Start,End)** and sets **Index** to **Start,** increments it in steps of 1 until **Index** is equal to **End.** For illustration another predicate **body()** is shown, which is not part of the loop construct.

```
/* a DO Index = Start,End   in steps of 1   */
/*                                          */
/* (does not test for Start > End)          */
/*                                          */
loop(End,End) :–body(End).
loop(Index,End):–body(Index),
                 Newindex is Index+1,
                 loop(Newindex,End).
body(Index) :–Index < 12, write(['In loop
                 at index = ', Index]), nl.
body(Index).
```

61

To ensure that loop continues to its conclusion of **Index** equal to **End** a second **body()** clause is included which is always true since it contains a variable and will match any call to **body()**. In the example the first clause of **body()** succeeds when **Index** is less than **12**.

The next example is similar to REPEAT UNTIL, but beware the effect of backtracking on the **body()** predicate.

```
loop :—repeat, read(X), body(X),
       X=:=stop.
```

The **read()** instantiates a term with **X,** the **body(X)** processes this term in some way, the test fails unless **X** is instantiated to **stop.** Backtracking begins, tries **body(X)** which perhaps also fails (if designed properly), cannot re-satisfy **read(X)** and reaches **repeat.** This succeeds, causing **read(X)** to be used next and so another cycle begins. Backtracking will be caused from the end of the clause until the final test succeeds.

Note, the following will *not* work:

```
a_bad_loop :—I is 1, repeat, I is I+1,
            body(I), I=:=10.
```

for the reason that **I** cannot be explicitly instantiated more than once in a clause. Only the system via backtracking can try alternative instantiations for a variable.

IF constructs may be set up using two separate clauses in a procedure such that when one fails the other is used,

```
if_test(X) :-condition(X), !, then_body(X).
if_test(X) :-else_body(X).
```

the *cut* prevents backtracking trying **else_body()** if initiated from **then_body.** A similar effect may be obtained using the OR connective semicolon (**;**) between clauses,

```
if_test(X) :-(condition(X), !, then_body(X);
              else_body(X)).
```

If available, the built-in operator $->$ automatically provides a satisfactory IF construct in Prolog,

P$->$**Q;R**   **P**$->$**Q**

The case **P**$->$**Q;R** means 'if P is true then Q else R', and the case **P**$->$**Q** means 'if P is true then Q else fail'. (Do not confuse the $->$ operator with the $-->$ operator which is used for grammar rule notation and is not described in this book.)

Examples

Assume the following have been loaded:

```
if_one(X) :-X==end -> write ('OK') ;
          write('not OK').
if_two(X) :-X==end -> write('OK') ;
          write('not OK'),
          write('another').
?- if_one(test).
not OK
yes
?-if_one(end).
OK
yes
?-if_two(test).
not OK another
yes
?-if_two(end).
OK
yes
```

Thus clauses, or sequences of clauses separated by commas, are selected on one side or the other of the semicolon depending upon the tested value of the condition before the -> symbols.

Brackets may be used to limit the scope of the construct,

```
....,(X==end -> write('one') ; write('two')),....
```

64

Lists and Strings

The following is an example of a list in Prolog notation:

[a,b,c]

Note the square bracket enclosing the list whose elements **a, b** and **c** are separated by commas.

Using lists

A list is an ordered sequence of elements which can have any length. It may grow or shrink during program execution as elements are added or deleted.

The elements of a list may be atoms, as in the example above, structures (*see* p.73) or other lists. Here are some examples,

[bill]
    a list of one element, atom **bill.**
[[bill,26],[colin,12]]
    a list which contains two lists **[bill,26]** and **[colin,12].**
[book, title(lisp),author(s_hughes)]
    is a list which contains the atom **book** and two structures **title(lisp)** and **author(s_hughes).**

The example with **bill** and **colin** may be a way of storing the ages of people associated with their names.

A list is a perfect example of a structure which is defined recursively, and may be manipulated very easily be recursive functions (*see* p.44 for recursion).

Formally, a list is defined thus:

A list is
  either an empty list which contains no elements
  and may be written [ ],
  or it contains two components a *head* and a *tail*.
  The *head* is the individual first element of the list.
  The *tail* is the remaining elements as a list.

Note: the head is an element.
      the tail is a list.
(This is exactly the same convention as Lisp adopts
using the CAR and CDR functions.)
  Core Prolog does not give any list manipulation
features other than the ability to separate off the
head and tail parts. Some basic functions for list
manipulation are given in the next section.
Prolog uses the notation, with variable **X** and **Y,**

[X|Y]

to match **X** with the head of a list and **Y** to the tail.
This result is obtained when an existing list is
matched with the **[X|Y]** argument in a predicate.
For example, the fact **memory** contains a list,

memory([a,b,c]).
?– memory([X|Y]).
X=a
Y = [b,c]
yes

Like atoms and other terms, lists do not just float
about in a Prolog program. They are defined in facts
and other clauses. Variables are used in lists for the
purposes of matching to defined elements, to build

66

Table 3 List matching

Original list	Required to match	Result instantiated
[a,1,b,2,c]	[X|Y]	X=a Y=[1,b,2,c]
[a]	[X|Y]	X=a Y=[ ]
[ ]	[X|Y]	fails
[a,b,c]	X	X=[a,b,c]
[a,b,c]	[X]	fails, incorrect syntax
[a,b,c]	[X,Y|Z]	X=a Y=b Z=[c]
[one,two]	[one|X]	X=[two]
[maureen,is],excellent]	[X|Y]	X=[maureen,is] Y=[excellent]
[maureen,is],excellent]	[[X|Y]|Z]	X=maureen Y=[is] Z=[excellent]

or decompose a list. Table 3 shows some combination of matching between lists (**X,Y,Z** are variables).

The mathematics of list processing, which was developed long before Prolog, uses a different and slightly more complex notation for lists. It involves a special operator, written as a full stop, called the dot-functor. In this notation the list **[a,b,c]** is,

   .(a,.(b,.(c,[ ])))

Such notation is shown using the **display** predicate (*see* p.35). Further details of this notation may be found in the Prolog literature.

List predicates

Below are examples of useful predicates for use with lists. The variables **L, L1, L2, L3** and **M** represent lists and **X,Y** elements.

```
/* APPEND append(L1,L2,L3) all lists      */
/* and L3=L1+L2                            */
   append ([ ],L,L).
   append ([X|L1],L2,[X|L3]) :—append
                                (L1,L2,L3).
```

An example of its use is

```
?— append ([a,b],[c,d],M).
M = [a,b,c,d].
yes
```

As with other Prolog predicates some goals may attempt to use the predicate in the reverse direction

to its definition. For example, given **L3** as **[c,d]**, what
are the values of **L1** and **L2**?

```
? append (L1,L2,[c,d]).
L1=[ ]
L2=[c,d]      ;          first solution, ask for
                         more

L1=[c]
L2=[d]        ;          second solution, ask for
                         more

L1=[c,d]
L2=[ ]        ;          third solution
no
```

A set of useful list predicates follows.

```
/* DELETE delete(X,L1,L2) deletes all X      */
/* from L1 giving L2                         */
   delete(_,[ ],[ ]).
   delete(X,[X|L],M) :–!,delete(X,L,M).
   delete(X,[Y|L1],[Y|L2]) :–delete(X,L1,L2).

/* EFFACE efface(X,L,M) removes the first */
/* occurrence of X from L giving M           */
   efface(_,[ ],[ ]).
   efface(A,[A|L],L) :–!.
   efface(A,[B|L],[B|M]) :–efface(A,L,M).

/* LAST last(X,[a,b,c,d,e]) gives X=e        */
   last(X,[X]).
   last(X,[_|Y]) :–last(X,Y).

/* MEMBER member(X,L) succeeds if X is */
/* in list L                                 */
   member(X,[X|_]).
   member(X,[_|Y]) :–member(X,Y).
```

```prolog
/* NEXTTO nextto(X,Y,L) succeeds if X    */
/* and Y are consecutive in L            */
   nextto(X,Y,[X,Y|_]).
   nextto(X,Y,[_|Z]) :-nextto(X,Y,Z).


/* REV rev(L1,L2) reverses list L1 into list */
/* L2                                         */
   rev(L1,L2) :-rev_add(L1,[ ],L2).
   rev_add([X|L],L2,L3) :-rev_add
        (L,[X|L2],L3).
   rev_add([ ],L,L).


/* SUBLIST sublist(L1,L2) L1 is a sublist    */
/* of L2 succeeds if every element of L1 is  */
/* in L2 consecutively.                      */
   sublist([X|L],[X|M]) :-prefix(L,M).
   sublist(X,[_|M] :-sublist(L,M).
   prefix([ ],_).
   prefix([X|L],[X|M]) ;-prefix(L,M).


/* SUBST subst(X,L,Y,M) M is made from  */
/* L with all X replaced by Y           */
   subst(_,[ ],_,[ ]).
   subst(X,[X|L],A,[A|M]) :- !,subst(X,L,A,M).
   subst(X,[Y|L]),A,[Y|M]) :-subst(X,L,A,M).
```

These list predicates are taken from *Programming in Prolog*, 2nd edn, by W. F. Clocksin and C. S. Mellish.
© Springer Verlag (1984) Berlin, Heidelberg, New York, London, Paris, Tokyo.

The following predicate performs an action very similar to the MAPCAR function in Lisp. It applies a predicate (instantiated with **P**) to every element of the list L giving modified elements in list M.

```
/* MAPLIST maplist(P,L,M) applies the     */
/* predicate P to each element of list L  */
/* giving list M                          */
maplist(_,[ ],[ ]).
maplist(P,[X|L],[Y|M]) :-Q=..[P,X,Y],call
                         (Q),maplist(P,L,M).
```

The **call()** predicate and **Q**=..**[ ]** which is the univ functor are described on p.84.

The predicate used with **maplist** has two arguments. The first is instantiated in turn with each element of the list, and the second is the result of the function to be placed in the output list.

In the example, **equality** has two clauses, each of which matches a specific atom.

```
equality(he,she).
equality(man,person).
equality(X,X).
?-maplist(equality,[he,is,the,top,man],L).
L=[she,is,the,top,person).
yes
```

71

Strings

Anything enclosed in double quotes is taken by
Prolog as a string, but within Prolog the string is
stored as a list of numbers. Each number is the code
for a character in the string. Using the **read**
predicate,

```
?—read(X).
"brian".
X=[98,114,105,97,110].
yes
```

where 98 is the ASCII code for **b,** 114 represents **r,**
and so on.

All the list manipulation predicates may be used to
modify the list of codes which forms a string, and
thus edit it as desired.

There is a rather useful function, **name,** which
may be used to convert between the name for an
atom and the list of character codes (i.e. a string).

name(A,L)

When **A** is instantiated to an atom name the result is
a list of character codes in **L.** This allows all the list
manipulation functions (given on p.69) to be used to
alter the string of characters.

```
?—name(brian,L).
L=[98,114,105,97,110].
yes
```

When **L** is instantiated to a list of character codes the result is an atom name in **A**. Thus any list, which was a symbol name and has been edited in list form, may be re-assembled as a symbol name.

```
?–name(A,[115,121,116,115,101,109].
A=system.
yes
```

In the following example the procedure **change** takes an atom name and creates a new one by appending the symbols **_own** to the end of it.

```
change(Name,Output):–name(Name,L),
  append(L,[95,111,119,110],M).
  name(Output,M).
?–change(method,X).
X=method_own
yes
```

The new atom name could be used to create a new clause using the univ functor (*see* p.84).

Data Structures

There are no global variables in Prolog programs. Data for general use by the program procedures is
- stored as facts, in what is called the database part of the program
- passed as parameters from procedure to procedure.

The types of data items available are atoms, lists and structures. The facts already discussed in this book are examples of simple one-level structures.

Structures

A one-level structure is a predicate, or functor, with a list of arguments (familiar already as a fact),

    pred(arg, arg, arg, ...).

The term functor is used for such a structure because there is a built-in predicate called **functor** which manipulates such structures (*see* p.83).

Example

book(dune, frank_herbert, gollancz).

Such a fact would satisfy a goal which enquired about the book with title **dune.**

?– book(dune, Author, Publisher).
Author=frank_herbert.
Publisher=gollancz.
yes

The arguments of a predicate may be any of the types atoms (as above), lists (as in the previous section) or predicates of the form,

    $pred_1$(arg,arg,$pred_2$(arg,arg),arg,...).

where $pred_1$ is a two level structure.

Example

book(dune,author(frank,herbert),
  gollancz).
?–book(dune,X,Y).
X=author(frank,herbert).
Y=gollancz.
yes

Predicates may be nested to any desired level, but two or three are generally sufficient. It may be useful to think of nested structures as being represented in tree structure form,

The following database and query illustrates a use of structure in obtaining specific information.

```
book(dune,author(frank,herbert),
  gollancz).
book(lisp,author(sheila,hughes),pitman).
book(exodus,author(moses),god).
?–book(X,author(Y,herbert),Z).
X=dune
Y=frank
Z=gollancz
yes
?–book(X,author(Y),Z).
X=exodus
Y=moses
Z=god
yes
```

Operators

An operator is a symbol, or a set of symbols, which represents a specific operation to be applied to one or more variables or constants.

For example, the arithmetic addition operator is the familiar + symbol, which appears between two expressions,

X+6   + is an INFIX operator

The logical operator **not** reverses the value of a boolean expression and appears before (to the left of) the expression,

not (X==stop)   **not** is a PREFIX operator

There are no common examples of an operator which comes after an expression. That is, a POSTFIX operator. In mathematics (but not Prolog) the ! symbol is used to indicate a factorial and appears as 6! or N!, so is a postfix operator.

Prolog provides a set of standard operators and also allows the programmer to define additional operators. Each operator has the following characteristics:

- position, given by PREFIX, INFIX, POSTFIX
- association, given by left or right (see below)
- priority, given by a numerical value

Standard operators

Core Prolog provides the set of standard operators shown in Table 5. Each Prolog implementation may use its own scale of values (e.g. 0 to 255) for operator priority, so Table 5 shows relative priorities. The characteristics of position and association are given by a slightly obscure notation known as the signature (Table 4). The **f** represents the position of the operator and the presence of **x,y** shows the expressions on which it operates.

Table 4 Operator signatures

Signature	Type	Comment
fx	PREFIX	
fy	PREFIX	may operate on itself
xf	POSTFIX	
yf	POSTFIX	may operate on itself
xfx	INFIX	
xfy	INFIX	right associative
yfx	INFIX	left associative
yfy	INFIX	

A **y** means the expression being operated upon can contain operators of the *same* or *lower* priority.

An **x** means the expression being operated upon can contain operators of *lower* priority only.

If the + operator was **xfy,** right associative, then,

X+Y+Z is taken as **X+(Y+Z)**

In fact, + is defined as **yfx,** left associative, so that,

X+Y+Z is taken as **(X+Y)+Z**

Table 5 Standard operators

Priority	Operators	Signature
HIGH		
↑		
	:- -->	**xfx**
	?-	**fx**
	; , ->	**xfy**
	not spy nospy	**fy**
	.	**xfy**
	$\{$ = \= == \== $\}$	
	=:= =\= < >	**xfx**
	=< >= **is** =..	
	+ -	**yfx**
	* / **mod**	**yfx**
↓	- or ~ (unary minus)	**fy**
LOW		

User-defined operators

In one sense, a user-defined operator is just another
way of writing a predicate symbol. As such, these
operators do not give any greater power to
programming than predicates themselves supply.
They tend to be used at the input and output parts of
a program to provide a 'natural' interface which
corresponds more closely with the problem solution.
However, such an interface smooths the
programming task and ultimately encourages more
intractable problems to be attempted, thereby

extending the general power of the Prolog language.

The predicate **op** is used to define an operator. Thus,

op(Priority, Signature, Name)

declares an operator **Name**. For example,

?– op(255, xfy, &).

declares the operator **&** to have priority 255 (which may be the highest in the system) and signature **xfy.** The signature indicates a right associative infix operator. So the factual details, such as the operators name, how it works and what priority it has, are supplied by **op.** But what does it do? Just as for any user predicate, the meaning of the operator is a matter for the programmer (*see* p.21). To illustrate this point a very simple program is written in three ways to show the movement in ideas from straightforward predicate form to operator form.

```
/* calculate the number of days in a year*/
days_in_year(Y,366) :–0 is Y mod 4,
                    not (0 is Y mod
                    100),!.
days_in_year (Y,365).
```

Execution gives

```
?– days_in_year (1987,X).
X=365.
yes
```

The second form of this program is

```
/* calculate the number of days in a year*/
are (days_in_year(Y),366) :-0 is Y mod 4,
                            not (0 is Y
                                mod 100),!.
are (days_in_year(Y),365).
```

Execution gives

```
?- are (days_in_year(1988),X).
X=366.
yes
```

Now define **are** as an infix operator and
days_in_year as a prefix operator.

```
/* calculate the number of days in a year*/
?- op(250,xfy,are).
?- op(200,fx,days_in_year).
days_in_year Y are 366 :-0 is Y mod 4,
                        not(0 is Y mod
                            100),!.
days_in_year Y are 365.
```

Execution gives

```
?- days_in_year 1989 are X.
X=365
yes
```

Essentially, **A are B** means **are(A,B)** and
days_in_year C means **days_in_year(C)**.

Note the goal symbol before each operator
declaration. The system must evaluate **op** before the
rest of the program is scanned so that it can be
interpreted in the correct way, with the operators
defined.

The following program illustrates the further use of operators.

```
/* Who does like someone and is          */
/* reciprocated?                         */
/* We will define two operators to make  */
/* the input and output nicely readable. */
?- op(230,xfy,'&').
?- op(220,xfy,'likes').
john likes mary.
john likes jane.
mary likes pete.
pete likes kate.
jane likes john.
kate likes pete.
brian likes _.
sheila likes _.
/* This is a package of actions which is a */
/* goal to be satisfied to solve the       */
/* problem. It could be given from the     */
/* terminal, but is convenient to          */
/* package up under the                    */
/* predicate 'wholovesyerbabe'.            */
wholovesyerbabe :-X likes Y, Y likes X,
    write (X&Y), nl,fail.
```

The last two 'facts' could be interpreted as brian likes everyone, and sheila likes everyone. Execution gives,

?–wholovesyerbabe.
john & jane
pete & kate
jane & john   and so on.

Metalogical Predicates

These built-in predicates have a common attribute in manipulating pieces of a Prolog program, rather than acting on variables directly. Examples of this type of predicate have been encountered in earlier sections; **assert** and **retract** (p.50), **call** (pp.42,71) and **name** (p.72).

The following group of predicates tst the type of the term instantiated to **X**:

var(X)   **nonvar(X)**

var succeeds for variable, **nonvar** for nonvariable.

atom(X)   **atomic(X)**   **integer(X)**

atom succeeds for atom only, **integer** succeeds for integer only, **atomic** for atom or integer.

The predicate **functor** allows the examination of a structure together with details of its arguments.

It may be used in another way to create a named structure.

functor(X,A,N)

If **X** is a compound term the effect is to instantiate **A** with the main functor and **N** with its arity (the number of arguments it contains).

Example

```
?- functor (a+b,A,N).
A=+ , N=2
yes
?- functor(max(X,Y,Z)A,N).
A=max, N=3
yes
?- functor ([a,b,c,d],A,N).
A=. , N=2        refer to p.68
yes
```

If **X** is not instantiated but **A** and **N** are, the appropriate structure is created,

```
?- functor(X,example,4).
X=example (_,_,_,_)
```

The predicate **arg** allows the selection of a specified argument from a structure.

arg(I,X,Y).

I specifies the argument, **X** is instantiated to the structure and the result is available in **Y.**

Example

```
?-
arg(2,book(dune,author(frank,herbert),
    gollancz),Y).
Y=author(frank,herbert).
```

The univ predicate, represented by the symbols =.. provides a means of creating a structure **X** from a list **L,** or obtaining all the arguments of a structure placed into the list **L.**

X=..**L.**

Example

```
?- X=..[one,a,b,c].
x=one(a,b,c).
yes
?- max(1,2)=..L.
L=[max,1,2,_12].
yes
```

The **call** predicate makes the Prolog system evaluate the argument as a goal. **call(X)** and **X** will have the same effect in most cases.

The **clause** predicate searches the program for a clause whose head is given.

clause(X,Y)

given the head of a clause **X** the body is instantiated with **Y.** If the clause has no body (is a fact†) then **Y** is given the value **true.**

Debugging Programs

A set of built-in predicates allow detailed
examination of the flow of execution control in a
Prolog program.

There is a useful model to enable the state of a
procedure to be understood during execution. This is
the Procedure Box Control Flow Model described
below.

Procedure Box Control Flow Model

The idea is that each time a procedure is invoked, a
box is imagined with a port at each corner (see
Figure 2). Each port represents a different way the
procedure may be entered or left.

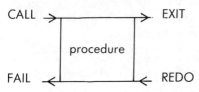

Figure 2 *Procedure box ports*

The CALL port is the port by which execution control
passes to the procedure on first invocation.

The EXIT port is the port by which execution control
leaves the procedure after successful invocation.

The REDO port is the port by which execution control
re-enters the procedure if it is to be re-satisfied
during backtracking.

The FAIL port is the port by which execution control leaves the procedure after unsuccessful invocation (it has failed).

Both **trace** and **debugging** with **spy** points will provide information identifying the appropriate port during the program execution.

Debug predicates

The basic tracing predicates are

trace   **notrace**

trace causes full tracing of program execution to be switched on. It remains on until **notrace** is given. The system will display a list of predicates and may include the information relating to the procedure box control flow model, that is the port; call, exit, redo, fail. If available a predicate **leash** will control the amount of detail given by the trace.

Further debugging is controlled by the predicates,

debug   **nodebug**   **debugging**

debug switches debug mode on, it remains on until **nodebug** is given. **debugging** displays information concerning the current state of debugging. In particular, this includes a list of spy points.

The operator **spy** stops the program execution when a named predicate is encountered. Both **spy** and **nospy** are defined as prefix operators.

spy X   **nospy X**

where **X** may be an atom or a predicate with indication of arity (the number of arguments) following the **/** symbol. For example,

spy max.
spy max/3.
spy brian/1

The arity is present to distinguish between definitions of the same predicate with different numbers of arguments. **nospy** cancels the given spy points. The port of the predicate is displayed when a spy point is encountered. Systems provide a range of simple instructions to control further execution. A typical set is

c continue	**s** skip	**p** print
	; redo	**t** trace
	r retry	**n** notrace

Appendix 1: Comparison with Other Variants of Prolog

A number of microcomputer-based implementations of Prolog follow the main parts of the 'core' Prolog which is described in this Handbook. For example, the Prolog-1 and Prolog-2 products of Expert Systems Ltd. However, the micro-Prolog of Logic Programming Associates Ltd, which is available for a wide range of microcomputers, differs somewhat from the syntax given here. Some major features of micro-Prolog are given below.

From IBM, for mainframe computers comes VM/ Prolog. It is an extensive implementation which has some features in common with the earlier Waterloo Prolog. Details are given on p.91.

Micro-Prolog

Micro-Prolog is an implementation of Prolog which runs on a range of microcomputers including the BBC micro, Sinclair Spectrum and many others which run the CP/M and MS-DOS operating systems. Its syntax differs from 'core' Prolog in that it is more like the notation used for Lisp programming. Basic micro-Prolog provides what is called a 'standard' syntax which is the basis for the comments given here. However, an additional module called SIMPLE may be loaded to provide a syntax based on a sentence-like form. Another module distributed with the system provides the DEC-10 style primitives which form the basis of the 'core' Prolog described in this book.

The following notes refer to 'standard' micro-Prolog.

- The form of clause (identied as a 'fact' on p.12) written as

   predname (term$_1$, term$_2$, ... term$_k$).

   becomes a list

   (predname   term$_1$ term$_2$ term$_k$)

The full clause form given on p.10 as

    Goal :– subgoal₁, subgoal₂, … subgoalₙ.

becomes a list of lists, since each of the Goal and subgoal terms is converted to a list in the manner shown for the 'fact'.

    ((Goal in list form) (subgoal₁ in list form) (....) (....))

Items in the lists are separated by a space.

- Variables are composed only from the letters **X,Y,Z,x,y,z,** to which may be appended an optional integer. Thus **X,x,y12** are distinct variables.

- The interpreter must be requested to prove a query against the current program by means of the **?** symbol. Without this the interpreter will add the new clause to the existing set. The standard system prompt is **&.** and the following examples illustrate the interpreter actions:

&. ((is_aged jane 45))

stores the (inner) list at the end of the current clauses. The equivalent 'core' Prolog statement would be

?– assertz (is-aged (jane, 45)).

Consider

&. ? ((has_descendant jane))

The result will be the system prompt **&.** if the clause succeeds and **?** if it fails. The value instantiated to **X** is not shown. If it is required it must be explicitly printed using the **pp** predicates as

&. ? ((has_descendant jane X) (pp X))

The equivalent 'core' Prolog statement would be

?- has_descendant(jane, Child).

and the output is shown on p.18.

- There are predicates which cover all of the actions provided by the 'core' predicates. However, the names are different and their semantics are generally also slightly different.
- The list notation using square brackets with commas separating the items, as shown on p.65, is not available. In micro-Prolog the | represents the dot functor which separates a head part and a tail part of a list. However, it does have a similar effect to the same symbol in 'core' Prolog when matching patterns against lists.

'Core' Prolog	Micro-Prolog
[a,2,ok]	(a 2 ok)
[a,[b,c]]	(a (b c))
[x,y|z]	(x y|z)

- The SIMPLE form of micro-Prolog uses 'sentences' rather than list notation.

SIMPLE	'Standard' micro-Prolog
$term_1$ Relation $term_2$	(Relation $term_1$ $term_2$)
term Relation	(Relation term)
term if $term_1$ and $term_2$	((term) ($term_1$) ($term_2$))

- Both forms of micro-Prolog use additional operators to control the amount of solution generated by a query. The operators FORALL, ISALL, are used in 'standard' and extended by the commands 'is' and 'which' used in SIMPLE.

VM/Prolog

VM/Prolog is an IBM implementation of the Prolog language. The product runs under the VM/SP operating system. It is written in assembler and comes complete with a powerful set of built-in predicates. It has an interface to Lisp/VM. The major difference with VM/Prolog and most other implementations is that it does not use 'core' syntax, but one that is similar to early versions of Waterloo Prolog.

The following differences have been identified between 'core' and VM/Prolog.

- Many of the predicates available in 'core' Prolog
  are not in VM/Prolog. This list includes **get, get0,
  display, skip, put, see, seeing, seen, tell,
  telling, told, nonvar, listing, asserta,
  assertz, clause, name.** The majority of these
  exist under other names or can be fairly readily
  generated using other predicates. On the other
  hand VM/Prolog includes many predicates which
  are not part of 'core' Prolog and which are
  needed by many programs.

- The following operations have different
  representations:

'core' Prolog	VM/Prolog	Meaning
:–	<–	if
?–	<–	query
;	|	or
,	&	and
!	/()	cut

- VM/Prolog is not sensitive to upper and lower
  case. Variables which would be represented as
  Var in 'core' Prolog are represented as ***Var** in
  VM/Prolog.

- The list notation using square brackets is not
  available by default. The standard notation of
  VM/Prolog represents the list **[a,b,c]** in the form
  (a.b.c.nil). To equate two variables with the
  head and tail of a list 'core' Prolog uses the
  notation **[A|B]** whilst VM/Prolog uses **(*A.*B).**

Consider the following VM/Prolog progam:

```
father(emma,chris).
mother(emma,anne).
parent(*X,*Y) <- (father(*X,*Y) |
   mother(*X,*Y)).
```

To request evaluation of the goal **parent (*X,*Y)**
type

```
<- parent(*X,*Y).
```

After echoing the goal as an acknowledgement
the system responds with the solution

```
1MS SUCCESS
<- PARENT(EMMA,CHRIS)
;                                request another solution
1MS SUCCESS
<- PARENT(EMMA,ANNE).
```

Appendix 2: Glossary of Terms

Arity   The number of arguments which a structure (or predicate) contains. An atom has no arguments and hence has an arity of zero.

Atom   An atom is a constant whose value is not exclusively numeric, e.g.

apple, send 14, 'FILE4'.

Body   The right-hand side of a clause. All the subgoals following the **:—** symbols.

Clause   A complete Prolog statement denoting either a fact or a rule. Begins with a predicate name and is terminated by a full stop. Comprises a head and a body.

Database   The set of facts in a Prolog program.

Fact   A clause without a body. Regarded as always true.

Functor   Used interchangeably with the term 'predicate'.

Goal   A goal is a term or a conjunction of terms formed using the **,** operator. When a goal is presented to the system, Prolog will attempt to prove that the goal can be satisfied.

Head   The left-hand side of a clause. The predicate part with arguments, before the **:—** symbols.

Instantiate   A variable is instantiated when it has been given an instance of some class of object. The object may be of type numeric or any other term which Prolog recognises.

List   A list is formed by the association of terms, using the list notation **[a,b,c].**

94

Operator   An operator is a special form for a predicate arity 1 or 2 acting in a similar way to conventional arithmetic operators.

Predicate   The name of the relation, occuring in the head part of a clause.

Procedure   A collection of clauses with the same predicate name.

Rule   Used interchangeably with the term 'clause'.

String   Strings are special cases of lists, where each element in the string has a single character as its value.

Structure   A structure is a single term, which consists of an organised collection of other terms. A structure is specified by its identifier and its arguments. The identifier is also called the predicate name or functor name. The identifier must be an atom, but the arguments may each be any valid type of term.

Term   May be a variable, an atom, an integer or a structure. Clauses and goals are special cases of terms, obeying certain rules of punctuation.

Unification   The act of matching terms. A pattern matching which provides the most general common instance between a goal clause and a clause to be matched with it.

Variable   A term whose value is initially undefined. In proving a goal, the value of the variable can be set to another term.

Appendix 3: Built-in 'Core' Predicates

The following list summarises the core predicates and their functions. For further details refer to the index and appropriate part of the book. Operators are given on p.76

abort	current execution abandoned, control returns to top level.
arg(I,X,Y)	the **I**th argument of term **X** is **Y**.
assert(C)	assert clause **C**.
asserta(C)	assert **C** as first clause.
assertz(C)	assert **C** as last clause.
atom(X)	term **X** is an atom.
atomic(X)	term **X** is an atom or integer.
call(X)	execute the procedure **X**.
clause(X,Y)	there is a clause with head **X** and body **Y**.
close(F)	close file **F**.
consult(F)	include clauses from file **F**.
debug	switch on debugging mode.
debugging	show debugging information.
display(X)	display **X**.
fail	cause backtracking.
functor(X,A,N)	principle functor of term **X** has name **A** and arity **N**.
get(X)	the next non-blank printable character input is **X**.
get0(X)	the next character input is **X**.
halt	exit Prolog.
integer(X)	the term **X** is an integer.
X is Y	**X** is the value of the arithmetic expression **Y**.

length(L,N)	the length of list **L** is **N.**
listing(X)	list the procedures **X.**
name(A,L)	the name of atom **A** is string(list) **L.**
nl	newline.
nodebug	switches off debugging mode
nonvar(X)	term **X** is not a variable.
nospy X	removes spy points from procedures **X.**
not(X)	succeeds if **X** fails.
notrace	switches off tracing.
op(P,S,N)	make atom **N** an operator of signature **S** and priority **P.**
print(X)	write the term **X.**
put(N)	the next character output is **N.**
read(X)	read term **X.**
reconsult(F)	updates the current program with clauses from file **F.**
repeat	succeeds repeatedly (during backtracking).
retract(C)	erase the first encountered clause **C.**
see(F)	make file **F** the current input stream.
seeing(F)	the current input stream is named **F.**
seen	close the current input stream.
skip(N)	skip input characters until **N** is found.
spy X	set spy points on procedures **X.**
tab(N)	output **N** spaces.
tell(F)	make file **F** the current output stream.

telling(F)	the current output stream is named **F.**
told	close the current output stream.
trace	switches on trace.
true	succeed.
var(X)	term **X** is a variable.
write(X)	write term **X.**
writeq(X)	write term **X** quoting names if necessary.
!	the cut.
,	and.
;	or.
−>	IF construct.
=..	univ functor.

Index

100

Computer Handbooks

Languages

Assembly Language for the 80286   Robert Erskine
Assembly Language for the 8086 and 8088   Robert
   Erskine
C Language   Friedman Wagner-Dobler
Structured Programming   Ray Welland
Lisp   Sheila Hughes
Introduction to Prolog   Brian Walsh

Business Applications

dBASE III   Peter Gosling
Framework and Framework II   Peter Gosling
Lotus 1–2–3   Dick Waller
Lotus Symphony   Dick Waller
Multiplan   Peter Gosling
SuperCalc and SuperCalc 2   Peter Gosling
VisiCalc   Peter Gosling

Microcomputers

The Amstrad 464, 664 and 6128   Boris Allan
The Apricot   Peter Gosling
The Sinclair QL   Guy Langdon and
   David Heckingbottom

Operating Systems

Introduction to Operating Systems
   Lawrence Blackburn and Marcus Taylor
The UCSD p-system   Robin Hunter

Word Processing

WordStar   Maddie Labinger and Jan Osborne
WordStar 2000   David Hawgood
Wordwise and Wordwise+   Wendy Chuter
Amstrad PCW8256 and PCW8512   David Hawgood

Pocket Guides

Programming

Programming   John Shelley
Statistical Programming   Boris Allan
BASIC   Roger Hunt
COBOL   Ray Welland
FORTH   Steven Vickers
FORTRAN   Philip Ridler
FORTRAN 77   Clive Page
LOGO   Boris Allan
Pascal   David Watt

Assembly Languages

Assembly Language for the 6502   Bob Bright
Assembly Language for the 8085   Noel Morris
Assembly Language for the MC 68000 Series
   Robert Erskine
Assembly Language for the Z80   Julian Ullmann

Microcomputers

Acorn Electron   Neil Cryer and Pat Cryer
Commodore 64   Boris Allan
Programming for the Apple   John Gray
Programming for the BBC Micro   Neil Cryer
  and Pat Cryer
Sinclair Spectrum   Steven Vickers
The IBM PC   Peter Gosling

Operating Systems

CP/M   Lawrence Blackburn and Marcus Taylor
MS-DOS   Val King and Dick Waller
PC-DOS   Val King and Dick Waller
UNIX   Lawrence Blackburn and Marcus Taylor

Word Processors

Introduction to Word Processing   Maddie Labinger
IBM Displaywriter   Jacquelyne A. Morison
Philips P5020   Peter Flewitt
Wang System 5   Maddie Labinger